100 YEARS OF HARLEY-DAVIDSON ADVERTISING

100 YEARS OF HARLEY-DAVIDSON ADVERTISING

Introduction by Jack Supple   Captions by Thomas C. Bolfert

Produced by Melcher Media
for Harley-Davidson Motor Company

Bulfinch Press
AOL Time Warner Book Group
Boston • New York • London

Harley-Davidson is the "Motor Company" because it originally sold motors for marine, commercial, or sport use as well as motorcycles. This is the Company's earliest known advertisement, which appeared in the January 2, 1905 issue of the *Cycle and Automobile Trade Journal*.

You can call it a brand, a cult, or a phenomenon, but it's much more than a motorcycle.

For 100 years, the burning legend of Harley-Davidson has been fanned by the winds of change and fueled by an American spirit of freedom, individualism, and the quest for adventure.

What William A. Davidson, Walter Davidson Sr., Arthur Davidson, and William S. Harley put together in the little work shed behind the Davidson house on Highland Boulevard in Milwaukee was more than a machine. It was the beginning of a way of life.

Even that long ago, it became apparent that Harley-Davidson® motorcycles had a unique emotional connection to the soul of its rider. What may have started as an economic alternative to the motorcar and a speedier conveyance than the bicycle soon took on a wind-in-the-hair sense of freedom and exhilaration. Early advertisements proclaimed "Get the most out of life" (1916) and "Get a kick out of life"(1925).

This thing was fun.

Oh sure, there would always be rational reasons to buy a Harley-Davidson. But what chance would competitors in other sports have compared to an ad that argued "Motorcycling: The Greatest Sport of Them All" (1931)? It's that timeless attraction, that sense of wanderlust, that's resonated deep in the genetic makeup of every freedom-loving rider on earth. It's what makes Harley-Davidson motorcycles relevant today in the lives of motorcyclists all over the world. The promise is simple and true: How you feel on a Harley® is like nothing else in the world.

Those who understand this best are Harley-Davidson's core customers, lovingly called the "Enthusiasts." They come from all walks of life, although they would prefer, thank you, to ride.

To see the faithful converge on their annual pilgrimage to Daytona or Sturgis is to see America's "melting pot" culture at its blast-furnace best. A lifelong member of Hell's Angels. An accountant from Atlanta. A group of riders from London. A retired couple from Michigan with their dog.

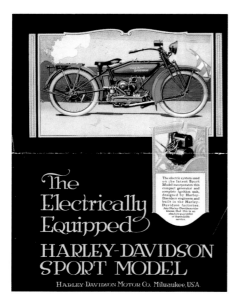

The Electrically Equipped HARLEY-DAVIDSON SPORT MODEL

HARLEY-DAVIDSON MOTOR CO. Milwaukee, U.S.A.

19**20**

The 37-cubic-inch Sport Model was offered in a WF version with a magneto or the WJ with a full electrical package. During the first decades of motorcycling, headlights and taillights, rather surprisingly, were optional equipment. If a model was not electrically equipped, the lights were acetylene powered.

19**70**

In 1969, Harley-Davidson factory racer Mert Lawwill won the #1 plate in AMA Grand National racing. The next year the red, white, and blue symbol became the unofficial company logo through most of the decade.

A CEO who would never be mistaken for a CEO. Six women, who teach school in Arizona, dressed in leather. A H.O.G.® chapter from Akron, Ohio. A newlywed couple from Germany. Some guy in buffalo horns.

What holds them together are their common values, shared with one another and with the Motor Company. Freedom. Individualism. The quest for adventure.

This deep and abiding sense of what Harley-Davidson represents to its customers has been the strength of the Motor Company, and maintaining that connection is one of its guiding principles. Throughout its history, whenever the Company forgot that central reason for its existence, its fortunes waned. But every time it reveled and celebrated in that connection to its customer, it would succeed.

It's the principle they would return to, time and again. Through wars and peacetime. Through ownership by AMF (American Machine & Foundry) and the buyback. Through Panheads, Knuckleheads, Shovelheads, Evolution®, Twin Cam 88s, and the Revolution V-Twin® engine. Through the introduction of the Harley Owners Group, MotorClothes Products™ and Genuine Motor Accessories, and an expansion of the brand's global appeal. Through it all, Harley-Davidson would strive to remain connected and loyal to its riders. Harley-Davidson's reward for this loyalty would be loyalty in kind.

Harley-Davidson is the one brand, the only brand, that is burned into the skin of its enthusiasts, the famous Bar & Shield tattoo second in the world only to "Mom." (Somehow, an advertisement in a magazine pales by comparison.)

Those of us who love the brand can only aspire to be Keepers of the Flame. We cannot create it, we can only tend it. The brand really belongs to the riders. The flame burns in their souls. In 2003, upwards of 500,000 of them will ride to Milwaukee to be part of the 100th anniversary pilgrimage. Similar celebrations will happen on five continents. The riders will heed the call from points all over the great wide world. Just to be a part of it. Just to feel the earth rumble.

Harley-Davidson may build it, but it's the riders' motorcycle. Their brand. Their way of life.

That's why when Willie G. Davidson and his styling team work on the next new bike design, they are just as likely to do it at a roadside rest stop surrounded by bikers as they are in the gleaming confines of the new Willie G. Davidson Product Development Center. When they're done, they will have created the newest incarnation of a legend. Just the sight of a Harley-Davidson pushes buttons deep inside the faithful. And the sound of it can make them downright misty-eyed.

Ads? Who needs ads?

It Is Not A Rational Decision.

19 88

Buying a motorcycle is rarely a rational decision. Instead, it is based on feeling, emotion, and a need to fill a certain void in one's life. While a small trailer may fill one's need for housing, a small motorcycle just doesn't fill that same need for a set of two wheels.

A Harley-Davidson motorcycle is the perfect advertisement. It grabs the eyeballs and pounds the eardrums and pushes a wake of attitude in front of it. A Harley has presence. It is impossible to ignore. The easy, loping potato-potato-potato of the V-Twin sets up some kind of harmonic between your pulse and red blood cells. The machine seems to know it has a soul, and when it intertwines with yours, you are hopeless to resist it.

By comparison, the attempts of we mere mortals to capture the mystique of Harley-Davidson in two-dimensional advertising may seem small and insignificant.

But over the years, Harley-Davidson Motor Company has found those ads that hit the mark, those that Harley-Davidson enthusiasts pull out of the magazine and hang on their garage walls, those that hit with a resonant "thump" deep in the chest. Such ads can do as much to reinforce the Harley-Davidson mystique as the next bike week at Sturgis, or a Saturday morning at the dealership, or a wave from a brother in the other lane.

It reaffirms who you are. Or who you want to be.

The advertising is for those who get it, whether they own a Harley-Davidson motorcycle yet or not. Don't chase those who don't understand. Don't exclude those who want to understand. We're not trying to sell you a Harley-Davidson.

We're trying to connect with the people who want to buy one. "It's not a rational decision" (1985).

So we thought you'd enjoy seeing the 100-year journey of Harley-Davidson Motor Company captured in the advertising signposts along the way. The people who work at the Motor Company engineered the dramatic turnaround that happened at Harley-Davidson in the 1980s. It was their drive, their spirit, their refusal to let this great name die. All the advertising was ever able to do was reflect the confidence they felt in the brand.

Historians can debate over when and how the brand caught on and became the legend that it is today. Moto-journalists will all have opinions about which Harley was the perfect combination of engineering and tradition to define (or redefine) its success. Advertising experts will argue over the potency of any given ad. But one thing is sure. As you page through the 100 years of Harley-Davidson advertising that follows, you will begin to experience that feeling unlike any other. Unless you're planning to buy your next Harley soon, you may want to take it a few pages at a time.

- Jack Supple
- Partner, Carmichael Lynch
- 2001

1912

As its product line grew to include both single-cylinder and V-Twin models, plus models that featured a new chain drive, Harley-Davidson's literature became more sophisticated. By 1912, the Motor Company was already capitalizing on its American heritage, featuring a handsome illustration of the nation's Capitol on a catalog cover.

1910s

The
ECONOMY
OF THE
MOTOR
CYCLE

HARLEY
DAVIDSON
MOTOR COMPANY
MILWAUKEE

1910

By 1910, Harley-Davidson production had soared to more than 3,000 units, all four-horsepower, single-cylinder models finished in Renault Gray with Carmine striping. In keeping with its increased output and growing reputation for quality, the Motor Company's literature featured detailed model specifications and excellent photographic reproductions.

1908

In June 1908, Walter Davidson, a naturally skilled rider and the Motor Company's first president, won the Federation of American Motorcyclists' prestigious 365-mile endurance run in the Catskill Mountains with a perfect score of 1000 points. A week later, riding the same stock motorcycle, he set a world economy record of fifty miles on one quart and one pint of gasoline.

MOTORCYCLES
AND THEIR COMMERCIAL USES

HARLEY-DAVIDSON
MOTOR COMPANY
MILWAUKEE, WIS.

1911

Very early on, it was apparent that there was a lucrative market for Harley-Davidson motorcycles as commercial vehicles. Less expensive to own and operate than automobiles, and able to navigate rutted roads better than a four-wheeled vehicle, motorcycles quickly became attractive to government agencies and private businesses alike.

1913

While this ad states that the five main points to consider when choosing a motorcycle are speed, economy, comfort, reliability, and durability, clearly the most important selling point in 1912 was speed. The twin-cylinder Model X-8-E boasted eight horsepower, an increase of more than twenty percent from the previous year.

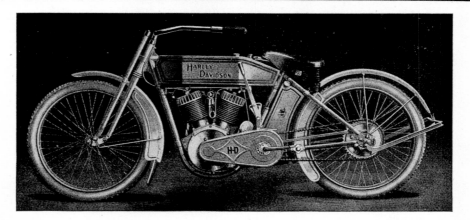

Sixty-eight Miles An Hour On a Harley-Davidson

IN buying a motorcycle there are five prime points to be considered. They are Speed, Economy, Comfort, Reliability and Durability. The Harley-Davidson has these qualities to a greater degree than any other motorcycle made.   Here's the proof:

Speed

In the Bakersfield, California Road Race, Frank Lightner's stock Harley-Davidson (the kind you can buy—not a special racing machine) attained a speed of 68 miles an hour.

Economy

The Harley-Davidson holds the World's Official Record for economy.

Comfort

The Harley-Davidson is the only motor-cycle which incorporates the Full-Floteing Seat and Free Wheel Control. The Ful-Floteing Seat places 14″ of concealed compressed springs between the rider and the bumps.   The Free Wheel Control permits the starting and stopping of the machine without the tiresome pedaling or running alongside common with the ordinary motorcycle.

Reliability

The Harley-Davidson is the only machine which has ever been awarded a diamond medal and a thousand plus five score in an endurance contest.   The plus five score was for its super-excellent performance. These awards were made by the National Federation of American Motorcyclists.

Durability

The first Harley-Davidson made, over eleven years ago, has covered now over one hundred thousand miles and is still giving satisfaction today, retaining even its original bearings.

Seven departments of the United States Government use a total of nearly 4000 of these machines.

This in itself is proof of its superiority. If you want a machine that will give and continue to give entire satisfaction from every point of view we would suggest that you call on our local dealer for demonstration or write for catalog.

HARLEY-DAVIDSON MOTOR COMPANY
PRODUCERS OF HIGH GRADE MOTORCYCLES FOR OVER ELEVEN YEARS

320 B Street   MILWAUKEE, WISCONSIN

HARLEY-DAVIDSON

1913

The narrative inside this brightly illustrated catalog cover from 1913 boasted that Harley-Davidson went from the smallest motorcycle manufacturer in the world to the largest producer of single-cylinder models in just over a decade. Despite more than doubling production of singles for 1913, nearly the entire production was sold out early for the year.

HARLEY-DAVIDSON

1914

Nearly eight thousand Model Fs with revolutionary two-speed transmission were produced in 1914. Developed by William S. Harley, the new transmission was an engineering masterpiece that combined the transmission, clutch, and brake in the rear hub. Approximately half of the Company's production that year was two-speed V-Twins.

HARLEY-DAVIDSON
1915

19**15**

The pioneering genius of William S. Harley, the Motor Company's first
engineer, was strikingly evident in 1915 with the introduction of the industry's first sliding gear three-speed transmission and modern clutch. The first
Model J, with its 61-cubic-inch, 11-horsepower V-Twin engine, elevated
motorcycling to a new level in power and performance.

19 16

With automobiles out of the reach of the common man, motorcycles became an affordable means of primary transportation for many. The addition of a sidecar expanded the versatility of the motorcycle by allowing riders to take the family along. By 1920, Harley-Davidson was selling over 16,000 sidecars annually.

1915

Recognizing the need to participate in organized racing on a factory level in order to garner publicity and build a reputation for performance, Harley-Davidson established its racing department in 1914. By the following year, the power and dependability of the Harley-Davidson motorcycle were rapidly becoming accepted facts as its riders scored repeated victories.

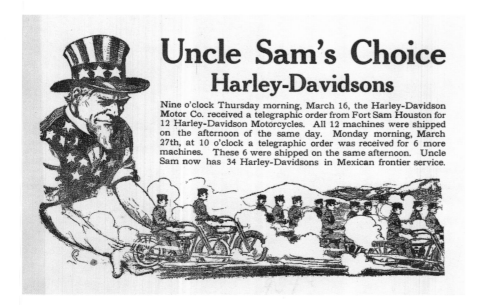

1916

When the U.S. Army had trouble catching Mexican bandit Pancho Villa after repeated raids on Texas border towns, they sent a telegram to Harley-Davidson headquarters in Milwaukee asking for motorcycles to help track him down. That day, the first of thirty-four Harley-Davidson motorcycles was sent by railcar to the Army. They didn't catch Villa, but the exercise hinted at the value of motorcycles in military service.

December, 1918

"To Battery E!"—"Yes Sir!"

WHEN the crisis came and the Army and Navy needed mounts that would carry an order with the speed of a "barked" command—mounts that would take punishment with the ruggedness of American morale—they turned to the motorcycle.

The Harley-Davidson

—in answer to the call—is now being made for the Government only, but some day we hope that you, too, may know the satisfaction of having in your personal service a motorcycle born in the same plant, groomed with the same care, and tuned up by the same testers as the one which at this moment may be tearing through a barrage to carry the report that "the 110th have taken . . . . . . "

Harley-Davidson Motor Company, Milwaukee, Wisconsin

"Ask the men in the service — they know."

1918

Harley-Davidson was eager to point out that civilians could own the same quality motorcycles as those used by the U.S. military in Europe. While its chief competitor, Indian, converted all its production to the military, Harley-Davidson wisely continued to devote more than half of its output to keeping civilian riders happy.

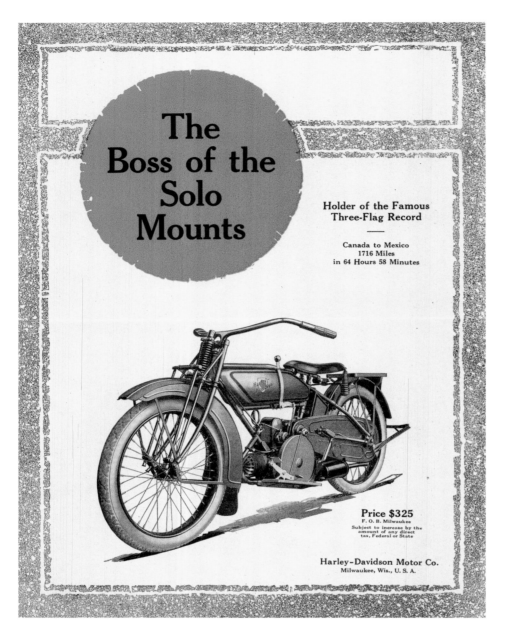

The Boss of the Solo Mounts

Holder of the Famous
Three-Flag Record
—
Canada to Mexico
1716 Miles
in 64 Hours 58 Minutes

Price $325
F. O. B. Milwaukee
Subject to increase by the
amount of any direct
tax, Federal or State

Harley–Davidson Motor Co.
Milwaukee, Wis., U. S. A.

1919

The Sport Model featured a unique engine, transmission, gas tank, front fork, and fenders unlike any previous Harley-Davidson model. It was relatively underpowered for its time, but nonetheless a smooth and reliable performer that handily set the Three-Flag record (Canada to Mexico) of over 1700 miles in just under sixty-five hours in 1919.

1919

Following World War I, there was renewed optimism as the country attempted to return to peaceful pursuits. Harley-Davidson sought to capture that feeling with colorful, airy illustrations that mirrored the style of the times and portrayed the motorcycle as sporty transportation.

By 1929, Harley-Davidson was producing nearly thirty thousand motorcycles for a network of dealers operating around the world. The following year, as the Great Depression took hold throughout the world, sales of new Harley-Davidson motorcycles dropped by a third.

1920s

Popular over the whole wide world!

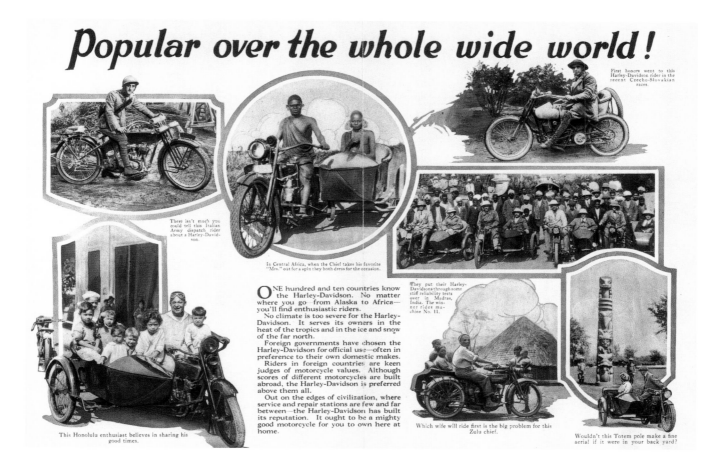

First honors went to this Harley-Davidson rider in the recent Czecho-Slovakian races.

There isn't much you could tell this Italian Army dispatch rider about a Harley-Davidson.

In Central Africa, when the Chief takes his favorite "Mrs." out for a spin they both dress for the occasion.

They put their Harley-Davidsons through some stiff reliability tests over in Madras, India. The winner rides machine No. 11.

This Honolulu enthusiast believes in sharing his good times.

ONE hundred and ten countries know the Harley-Davidson. No matter where you go—from Alaska to Africa—you'll find enthusiastic riders.

No climate is too severe for the Harley-Davidson. It serves its owners in the heat of the tropics and in the ice and snow of the far north.

Foreign governments have chosen the Harley-Davidson for official use—often in preference to their own domestic makes.

Riders in foreign countries are keen judges of motorcycle values. Although scores of different motorcycles are built abroad, the Harley-Davidson is preferred above them all.

Out on the edges of civilization, where service and repair stations are few and far between—the Harley-Davidson has built its reputation. It ought to be a mighty good motorcycle for you to own here at home.

Which wife will ride first is the big problem for this Zulu chief.

Wouldn't this Totem pole make a fine aerial if it were in your back yard?

1920

As its reputation for power and dependability grew, the Harley-Davidson motorcycle soon became popular in nearly every developed country in the world—and even in some not so developed. From the Arctic to the tropics, Harley-Davidson's motorcycles were often the choice of riders and governments alike.

1920

Harley-Davidson hoped to attract both boys and girls to its product line by offering as many as nine distinctly different bicycle models. The bicycles were made of the highest quality materials and painted the same trademark olive green as the motorcycles, but never achieved the same degree of loyalty and success as the company's motorcycles.

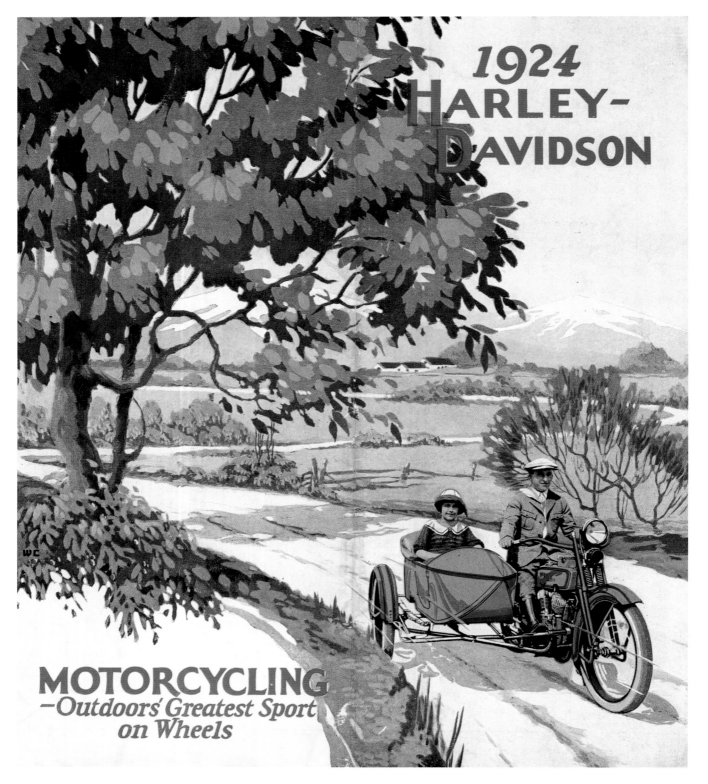

1924 HARLEY-DAVIDSON

MOTORCYCLING
—Outdoors' Greatest Sport
on Wheels

1924

With the introduction of the assembly line in production, some automobiles became as inexpensive as motorcycles. As a result, Harley-Davidson concentrated more on the sporting aspect of motorcycling rather than on its utility.

1925

Fresh country air, the freedom of the open road, and a day with fellow enthusiasts were lures of early motorcycling. The 1925 models sported a new "Stream-Line" teardrop gas tank, which gave them a sleek, modern look. The teardrop tank, since updated, has remained a part of the classic Harley-Davidson look to this day.

You'll find your Harley-Davidson dealer a regular fellow. He is the sort of a man you like to know and do business with. He's an old rider and knows just what you want. He is equipped to take care of your needs—and to see that you get every mile of service out of the machine that we build into it at the factory.

Drop around to your dealer and say "howdy," and then let him give you a ride with the 1925 model. If you can't get to see him right away, mail him the postcard. You'll get the 1925 catalog in a hurry, that tells all about the new Harley-Davidson.

Your dealer is your kind of a man—get in touch with him today!

HARLEY-DAVIDSON MOTOR CO.
MILWAUKEE
U. S. A.

Get a kick out of Life with a **HARLEY-DAVIDSON**

1925

As early as 1925, Harley-Davidson was extolling the virtues of its worldwide dealer network as a solid link between the factory and the rider. The Harley-Davidson dealer was always ready to meet the needs of the rider, providing parts, service, fellowship, and a meeting place to gather with other Harley-Davidson enthusiasts.

1927

Harley-Davidson's aim for model development has always been one of gradual evolution. This flyer for the 1927 Model J, which featured the venerable F-head motor, with a new circuit breaker to replace its distributor, explained the improved performance and reliability in wet weather.

1928

Two-cam racing motors had been avilable from Harley-Davidson on
a limited basis for nearly a decade when the company introduced street versions in 1928. The Two Cam Twins, available in 61- and 74-cubic-inch
versions, were some of the fastest street models of their day but were only
produced for two years.

1929

The thrill of a powerful Harley-Davidson motorcycle on a country road was
the theme of this famous 1929 illustration, which was used both as a poster
and as literature art. The long-running, 45-cubic-inch flathead twin
debuted that year and was used in production through the 1973 model year.
Every 1929 model featured a pair of bullet headlights.

1931

As the Great Depression gradually tightened its grip on the nation and the world, Harley-Davidson touted motorcycling as the greatest sport of all in an attempt to attract buyers from other pursuits. In 1931, sales dropped more than forty percent from the previous year and sixty percent from two years earlier.

1930s

The Harley-Davidson Bar & Shield logo has been a symbol of high-quality, dependable motorcycling for over ninety years since its introduction. Changing and evolving over the decades, the venerable Bar & Shield has undergone many refinements but stands today as one of the most recognizable marks in the world.

Genuine Harley-Davidson Enthusiasts From the World Over

This 26-Year Old Trade-Mark Stands for Quality Motorcycles

All 1929-30 Harley-Davidson models featured a pair of small, bullet-shaped headlights. They were touted as improved lighting, but they were more of a styling exercise than a functional improvement; it soon became apparent that a single large headlight was superior, and Harley-Davidson dropped the dual headlights in 1931.

1930

Colorful illustrations were once a mainstay of Harley-Davidson advertising. Motorcycle and passengers would often be presented in romantic illustrations. Here, the well-dressed gentleman rider and his flapper companion enjoy a mountain vista.

1930

Harley-Davidson experimented with different looks in 1929 and 1930 when it introduced dual headlights and unusual mufflers. The '29s had a peculiar four-tube, dual-exhaust system that was changed to a two-tube, single-exhaust system the following year.

1933 (Next Page)

The Motor Company offered unadvertised color combinations in the early thirties in a departure from its standard olive paint, but it wasn't until 1933 that Art Deco tank logos and striking two-tone color combinations became the norm. Black and Mandarin Red, as well as three other brilliant combinations, were available to riders that year.

BLACK AND
MANDARIN RED

THE 1933 HARLEY·DAVID

ON 74 BIG TWIN MODEL

19**35-37**

By 1936, America was struggling through the Great Depression, and people were anxious to forget their financial worries, one of which was a shortage of money. Harley-Davidson offered a way to enjoy the beauty of the land in an inexpensive, exciting way—from the saddle of a powerful V-Twin motorcycle from Milwaukee.

HARLEY-DAVIDSON 61 OHV

Sensation of the Motorcycle World

Bill Cummings, winner of the 500-Mile Indianapolis Automobile Speed Classic in 1934 and third place winner in 1935, gets a tremendous kick out of owning and riding this white 61 OHV. It's the kind of a motorcycle champions like.

Minus fanfare and ballyhoo, a new motorcycle has come on the scene and has taken the world by storm. Wherever shown, wherever ridden and owned, the new 61 OHV Harley-Davidson has caused a sensation. Here is a NEW motorcycle incorporating ideas the seasoned rider gives his immediate and unqualified approval. As one owner writes, "It's my dream come true."

From everywhere come the most enthusiastic praises for this super motorcycle. Its wonderful handling qualities, its snappy response, its ability to stand up and "take it" make this 61 OHV the outstanding motorcycle of today and the motorcycle of tomorrow. See this great motorcycle at your dealer's and put it through its paces.

HARLEY-DAVIDSON MOTOR CO., *Milwaukee, Wis., U.S.A.*

1936

Harley-Davidson took a major gamble when it introduced the revolutionary 1936 Model EL during the darkest days of the Great Depression. Because of ongoing developmental issues, the EL did not appear in model literature until late in 1936.

HARLEY-DAVIDSON MOTORCYCLES FOR 1937

1937

The acceptance of the all-new 1936 EL—the only model that year to boast a new teardrop gas tank, double-loop frame, and horseshoe oil tank among other features—prompted the proliferation of these advancements throughout the entire product line for 1937. Many of these features are still in evidence in the new models of today.

HARLEY – DAVIDSON

for 1938

The open road is calling — the magic of mountains, plain, and seashore awaits your exploration. Happy motorcycle club boys and girls welcome you to their tours and runs and invite you to take part in their good times. Back and forth to work, evening trips, weekend jaunts, vacation tours — your Harley-Davidson brings you healthful outdoor sport and economical transportation. Swing into the saddle and enjoy Motorcycling — The World's Greatest Outdoor Sport!

| 1938

Through the thirties and forties, organized club rides were common in the world of motorcycling. As the nation struggled out of the Great Depression, Harley-Davidson invited people to take part in the good times enjoyed by club members in their runs, rallies, and racing events.

1942

Despite converting most production to the war effort in 1942, Harley-Davidson was still able to produce a small number of motorcycles for civilian, police, and commercial uses.

1940s

1941

With the economic hardships of the thirties abating, Harley-Davidson prepared for a new decade by announcing a handful of improvements and a new model for 1941. The first FL model, featuring a Motor Company first overhead value 74-cubic-inch engine, made its debut just in time to be blunted by America's entrance into World War II.

THE 1941 HARLEY-DAVIDSON

Come in – See – Ride . . . .

New clutch design on all models • Centrifugally-controlled oil pump on all models • Improved 45 transmission • New Big Twin muffler • Airplane-style speedometer face • New front brake hand lever • Stainless steel tank strips • Larger air cleaner • Redesigned radio carrier on police models • Many other improvements • New 74 OHV model • Beautiful color options • Lower prices on 61 OHV and 45 WLDR

FOR TOPS IN FUN RIDE A '41

1941

During World War II, much of the nation's industrial might focused on the war effort, so Harley-Davidson motorcycles were utilized for home defense and by many of the Allied nations in their war efforts. Harley-Davidson was fortunate to be able to build its core product during the war—unlike some manufacturers—and produced over 90,000 motorcycles for the Allies as well as a modest number for domestic enforcement.

1942

The 45-cubic-inch WLA was the workhorse of the Allied military forces and saw service in many foreign armies, including those of Canada, Russia, New Zealand, and China, as well as all branches of the U.S. military.

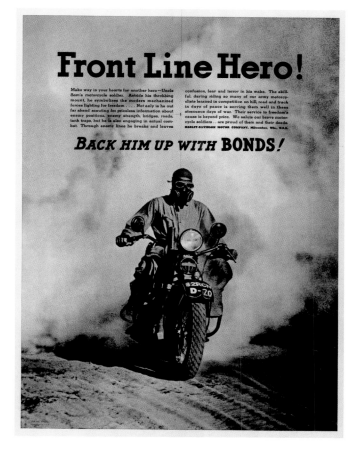

The World's Finest Motorcycle...

HARLEY-DAVIDSON

THE MIGHTY

HARLEY-DAVIDSON

...WORLD'S MOST POPULAR MOTORCYCLE!

1947–48

While the European motorcycle manufacturers struggled to rebound following the war, Harley-Davidson enjoyed renewed sales, especially with the powerful and more technologically advanced Panhead engine introduced in 1948. Sales soared to nearly thirty thousand units that year, as riders once more took to the open road.

MAKE YOURS A Hydra-Glide VACATION

for the time of your life...

FOR the grandest vacation you ever had, swing into the saddle of a Hydra-Glide Harley-Davidson. Pack the saddle bags, take a friend on the buddy seat, fill up with gas and oil and you're off on a thrilling, fun-packed trip you will never forget. You'll ride all day and, if you wish, far into the night and still feel like going on and on. You'll glide over endless tar lines and over rough spots. You'll hit bumpy side roads and country lanes with barely a quiver. Gone is that old feeling of fatigue. After a day of hundreds of miles of travel, you'll wake up the next morning fresh as a daisy — eager to get going and see more of this great country of ours.

The places you thought were too far away for a trip of a week or two are now within easy reach. Yellowstone, Yosemite, Carlsbad Caverns, California,

Black Hills, Florida, our Nation's Capital, Niagara Falls, and scores and scores of other scenic spots beckon you to come. You'll see more and you'll explore more with your Harley-Davidson Hydra-Glide. The miles will slip past all too soon as you glide along with effortless ease, taking in the panorama of scenery you will never forget. What a wonderful time will be yours! What a truly magnificent, unforgettable vacation you will have!

Resolve to make this year's vacation the best you've ever had. Let your Harley-Davidson dealer give you a Hydra-Glide ride. Get the feel of the smoothest ride you ever experienced on two wheels. Then, with a Hydra-Glide, your vacation will be the best you've ever had — one you will want to tell about and that will bring back pleasant memories for years and years.

HARLEY-DAVIDSON MOTOR COMPANY • MILWAUKEE 1, WIS., U.S.A.

HARLEY-DAVIDSON

1949

Motorcycling changed forever with the introduction of the Hydra-Glide front forks in 1949. Gone on the Big Twin models was the springer front end, replaced instead with gracefully tapering hydraulic front forks that have since become a Harley-Davidson trademark. While many riders initially referred to the bike as a Hydra-Glide, it wasn't until several years later that its name became official.

1954

Harley-Davidson celebrated its golden anniversary with special bronze medallions on the front fenders of all its models. While it is generally accepted that the Motor Company had its origins in 1903, the fiftieth anniversary medallions didn't appear until the 1954 model year. In order to stimulate sales, Harley-Davidson offered test rides and easy payment plans.

1950s

1949–50

Recognizing the crucial link between the factory and the rider, the Motor Company maintained a close relationship with its dealer network from the start. Harley-Davidson not only encouraged dealers to hold open houses in the late forties and early fifties to welcome riders into their stores, but was eager to point out the features of its models, including the economy of its lightweight bikes.

SAFE, MODERN
Power Riding
FOR EVERYONE
at Low Cost

yours
FOR HAPPY DAYS

The New, Brilliant

HARLEY-DAVIDSON 125

with road-cushioning

Tele-Glide Fork

1950–52

Introduced in 1948, the Model S was an American version of the German DKW, which the United States had permission to reproduce domestically as part of the War Reparations Act following World War II. The 1952 version had big bike styling and appealed to both younger riders and those seeking fun, economical transportation.

be a **big wheel** in motorcycling

become a member of the HARLEY-DAVIDSON mileage club

What it is

The Mileage Club is sponsored and was organized by the Harley-Davidson Motor Co. to officially recognize loyal Harley-Davidson riders who have reached specific mileages on their Harley-Davidsons since January 1, 1950. The mileage can be made on one or more Harley-Davidsons, and the motorcycles need not necessarily be owned by the rider.

Who can join

Those riders who have ridden their Harley-Davidsons 25,000 miles or more, 50,000 miles or more, or 100,000 miles or more since January 1, 1950, are eligible to join the Mileage Club in any one of the three groups. As soon as your mileage makes you eligible for any one of the three groups, go to your Harley-Davidson dealer and have him certify your official application. Motorcycle police officers and commercial riders of Harley-Davidsons they do not personally own are, of course, also eligible. Only those applications signed and submitted by a Harley-Davidson dealer will be accepted.

What membership means to you

You're going to be a mighty proud rider when you receive your official pin and membership card for the mileage group you qualified in: Those in the 25,000-mile group will receive a beautiful bronze pin and a blue membership card signed by President W. H. Davidson of the Harley-Davidson Motor Co.; those in the 50,000-mile group will receive an attractive rose-gold pin and a light green card signed by President Davidson; and those special folks who reach that 100,000-mile goal will receive a bright gold pin and a distinctive gold-colored membership card signed by President Davidson. Be the big wheel in *your* group—become a member of the Harley-Davidson Mileage Club as soon as you can.

HARLEY-DAVIDSON MOTOR CO., MILWAUKEE 1, WIS., U. S. A.

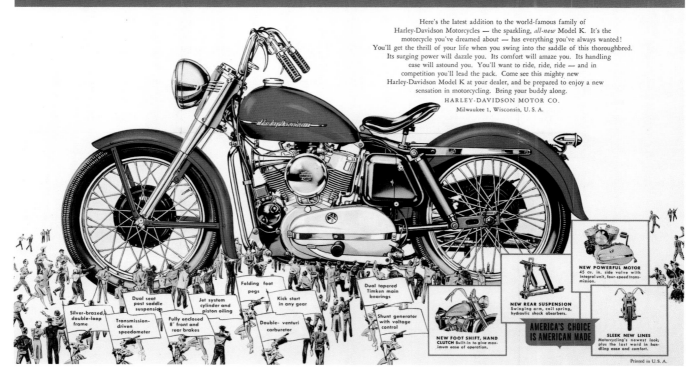

Presenting — America's Most Sensational Motorcycle!

THE NEW HARLEY - DAVIDSON Model K

designed to outperform, outride, outlook, outvalue ... any motorcycle in its class!

Here's the latest addition to the world-famous family of Harley-Davidson Motorcycles — the sparkling, *all-new* Model K. It's the motorcycle you've dreamed about — has everything you've always wanted! You'll get the thrill of your life when you swing into the saddle of this thoroughbred. Its surging power will dazzle you. Its comfort will amaze you. Its handling ease will astound you. You'll want to ride, ride, ride — and in competition you'll lead the pack. Come see this mighty new Harley-Davidson Model K at your dealer, and be prepared to enjoy a new sensation in motorcycling. Bring your buddy along.

HARLEY-DAVIDSON MOTOR CO.
Milwaukee 1, Wisconsin, U. S. A.

1952

In 1952, a totally new Harley-Davidson model made its appearance to compete with the fast and nimble models from Britain. The 750cc Model K, with its compact engine and transmission, hand-operated clutch, short wheelbase, and sporty looks, became an instant success—despite not measuring up to the performance of its competitors.

1952

The Mileage Club was founded in 1951 to recognize riders who had clocked 25,000, 50,000, or 100,000 miles since January 1, 1951. Remarkably, seventy-three members had earned their 100,000 mileage pins and membership cards by the Club's fourth year.

AGAIN
JOE LEONARD and HARLEY-DAVIDSON "K" WIN
20-MILE NATIONAL CHAMPIONSHIP
FOR ONE-MILE TRACKS
1st. JOE LEONARD-"K" 2nd. PAUL GOLDSMITH-"K"
3rd. CHARLIE WEST-"K"
TIME: 14-MINUTES 5.25 SECONDS NEW A.M.A. RECORD
JOE LEONARD
BAY MEADOWS, CALIFORNIA, JULY 25, 1954

AGAIN
AMERICA'S GREATEST SPEEDWAY CHAMPIONSHIP
LANGHORNE – 100-MILER
GOES HARLEY-DAVIDSON
EVERETT BRASHEAR, 1st
RAY GOFF, 2nd...JOHN HOOD, 3rd...ALL "K's"
* NEW RECORD 66 MINUTES, 6.15 SECONDS
25-MILE AMATEUR Won by BRAD ANDRES on "K"
LANGHORNE, PENNSYLVANIA, SEPTEMBER 5, 1954
EVERETT BRASHEAR
BRAD ANDRES

LACONIA – GRAND SLAM for HARLEY-DAVIDSON !
JOE LEONARD WINS 100-MILE NATIONAL ON "K"
TIME – ONE HOUR, 51 MINUTES, 3.91 SECONDS...NEW TRACK RECORD
BILL MEIER WINS 50-MILE AMATEUR ON "K"
TIME – 55 MINUTES, 31.60 SECONDS.......... NEW TRACK RECORD
HERB REYNOLDS WINS 25-MILE NOVICE ON "K"
LACONIA, N.H. – ONE-MILE ROAD RACE COURSE – JUNE 20, 1954
Silk Screen Printed in U.S.A.

JOE LEONARD

1954

While the 750cc flathead K Model was making its mark on the nation's
streets, the KR racing version was sweeping the nation's tracks in the early
fifties. The KR dirt track racers (and later the road racers) went on to virtu-
ally dominate the American racing scene until the end of the sixties, when
the overhead valve racing era began.

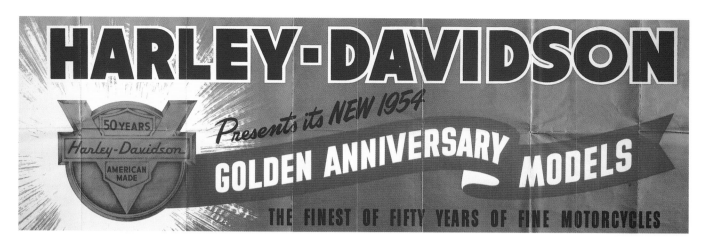

19**54–55**

All the 1954 models carried a handsome bronze medallion on the front fender boasting "50 years, American made." In 1955, Harley-Davidson had the most complete lineup of motorcycle models in the world. Harley-Davidson had something for every two-wheeled enthusiast, from 125 and 165cc two strokes to touring and sport bikes, plus Servi-Cars and sidecar rigs for those seeking a third wheel.

19**56** (Next Page)

The 750cc Model K was an instant success when it debuted in 1952. The K model evolved into the faster 883cc KH in 1954, but the KHK version, with racing cams and polished heads, set the pace for this model line.

Ride the Record

HARLEY

1956

Adventure ahead

74 OHV HARLEY-DAVIDSON
'57 HYDRA-GLIDES

MODEL FL

FIRST CHOICE IN AMERICA . . . THE SUPERLINER FL

You're *way ahead* with a Hydra-Glide® . . . on the expressways and byways of America. *Way ahead* for sheer luxury . . . way ahead for thrilling power . . . way ahead for dependability. Here is motorcycling enjoyment . . . plus! Sure, steady power coupled with a smooth, gliding ride. Wherever you find motorcyclists . . . you'll find Hydra-Glides® outnumbering all others by a wide margin. It's *first* in America . . . and the finest in the world!

AHEAD...WAY AHEAD WITH THE SUPER-POWERED FLH

For the rider who wants to be a leader among leaders . . . it's the power-packed FLH with that extra *thrust!* Up to sixty horsepower is compactly contained in this sensational Hydra-Glide® . . . poised and ready to deliver a whole new world of thrilling experiences at the flick of a wrist. You'll tingle at the unbelievable, surging "take-off" of this custom-built model. Words can't begin to describe the riding sensations of the Hydra-Glide® FLH. Your first ride will tell you . . . you'll be *way ahead* with an FLH in '57.

MODEL FLH

HARLEY-DAVIDSON MOTOR CO.
Milwaukee 1, Wisconsin, U. S. A.

FLH FEATURES

1. *How the FLH gets its GO. Cylinder head showing super-polished intake ports.*

2. *Attractive shield emblem on the oil tank sets you apart as the owner of a custom-built FLH Model.*

3. *New FLH aluminum alloy piston, with new, power-retaining narrow compression rings. Compression ratio increased to 8 to 1.*

4. *FLH, high-lift "Victory" cam results in greater horsepower and acceleration.*

FOR ALL HYDRA-GLIDES

5. *Smooth operating, multiple dry disc clutch. Built for rugged use—high torque capacity, dependable.*

6. *Stop! Safe, sure internal expanding brakes, front and rear. Fully enclosed and waterproof.*

7. *The famous Hydra-Glide® fork produces the perfect ride. Hydraulically-controlled spring fork does the work.*

8. *New, improved push rods permit greater amount of rod adjustment and result in easier removal of push rods in service work.*

FEATURES

NEW, MORE DURABLE H-D 100 FINISHES

New formula enamel stays better looking . . . longer. Needs no waxing. Resists scratches and dents. Luxurious color selection: Skyline Blue, Birch White, Pepper Red, Black, Metallic Midnight Blue (extra cost).

OLD PUSH ROD

NEW PUSH ROD

8

6

5

4

1957

With the Indian Motorcycle Company closing a few years earlier, Harley-Davidson emerged as the sole manufacturer of large touring motorcycles by the mid-fifties. Despite the hardtail frame, the Hydra-Glide was the epitome of Harley-Davidson touring motorcycles in 1957. The next year, a vastly more comfortable ride was introduced with the rear suspension featured on the Big Twins.

TOMORROW'S THRILLS TODAY!

A NEW MOTORCYCLE FOR THE MAN OF ACTION

Yours today . . . right now . . . all the exciting, riding experiences you've ever dreamed of . . . all wrapped up in the sweetest chrome-and-enamel power package ever produced . . . the new Harley-Davidson overhead . . . the SPORTSTER! Yours today . . . engineering, design and performance that will make you forget the riding thrills of yesterday and have you eagerly looking forward to the next ride on your new SPORTSTER.

To you . . . from the makers of the finest OHV's in the world . . . comes this sparkling, new, action-packed overhead. How about a ride?

HARLEY-DAVIDSON MOTOR CO.
MILWAUKEE 1, WIS., U.S.A.

1957 HARLEY-DAVIDSON
SPORTSTER

A combination that's hard to beat . . . the best ride in motorcycling coupled with the newest, most exciting engine in motorcycling.

Engineered from tip to taillight to provide you, the rider, the ultimate in mechanical performance and riding pleasure.

Check the many SPORTSTER superior features. Take a long look at its glistening beauty and trim lines. See it — ride it! Make your next move . . . up!

Own and ride a new Harley-Davidson SPORTSTER!

left broadside   *right broadside*

NEW MORE DURABLE "H-D 100" FINISHES
New formula enamel stays better looking . . . longer. Needs no waxing. Resists scratches and dents. Luxurious color selection. Skyline Blue, Birch White, Pepper Red, Black, Metallic Midnight Blue (extra cost).

FOR THE SPECTACULAR IN SMOOTH RIDING

Smooth operating, seven-plate clutch is sturdy and dependable. Built for thousands of trouble-free miles, it makes the SPORTSTER ride smooth and effortless.

Rear swinging arm suspension and large diameter shock absorbers result in the finest ride in motorcycling. Chrome covers add to SPORTSTER good looks.

Easy riding hydraulic front fork. Long, helical springs in the main tubes are hydraulically controlled with hydraulic stops on both the recoil and cushion positions.

Low frame, low saddle position produces a comfortable riding position and makes the SPORTSTER a pleasure to ride and easy to handle on or off the road.

1957

In 1957, a new Harley-Davidson model roared into the motorcycle world. The 883cc Sportster, with its overhead valve engine and integral 4-speed transmission, gained rapid acceptance on America's roads and is generally acknowledged as the first of the superbikes.

NEW JET-SILHOUETTE

HARLEY-DAVIDSON
SPORTSTERS FOR '61

Nestled under the tail of a Voodoo jet fighter, Harley-Davidson proudly presented its two Sportster models for 1961. Dressed for sport touring, the H on the left sports hard bags, windshield, two-up seat, and a four-gallon gas tank. The fast and nimble CH on the right is ready for street or trail with its high exhaust pipe and sport handlebars.

1960s

1960

The 1960 Duo-Glide was offered in four versions. The high-compression Super Sport was available in hand shift or foot shift, as was the lower compression Sport Solo. All could be ordered in Hi-Fi Red, Blue, or Green, with white accents and a full complement of accessories including colored windshields, bumpers, deluxe saddle, and a host of chrome add-ons.

1960

Skyline Blue and white or black and white were the stock colors of the 1960 lineup of lightweight, sport, and touring models from Harley-Davidson. However, it was the nearly iridescent Hi-Fi colors of Red, Blue, or Green that really made them stand out.

DUO-GLIDE FL

DUO-GLIDE FLH

SPORTSTER XLH

SPORTSTER XLCH

Stand out in '60

WITH A

NEW HARLEY-DAVIDSON

SUPER-10

TOPPER

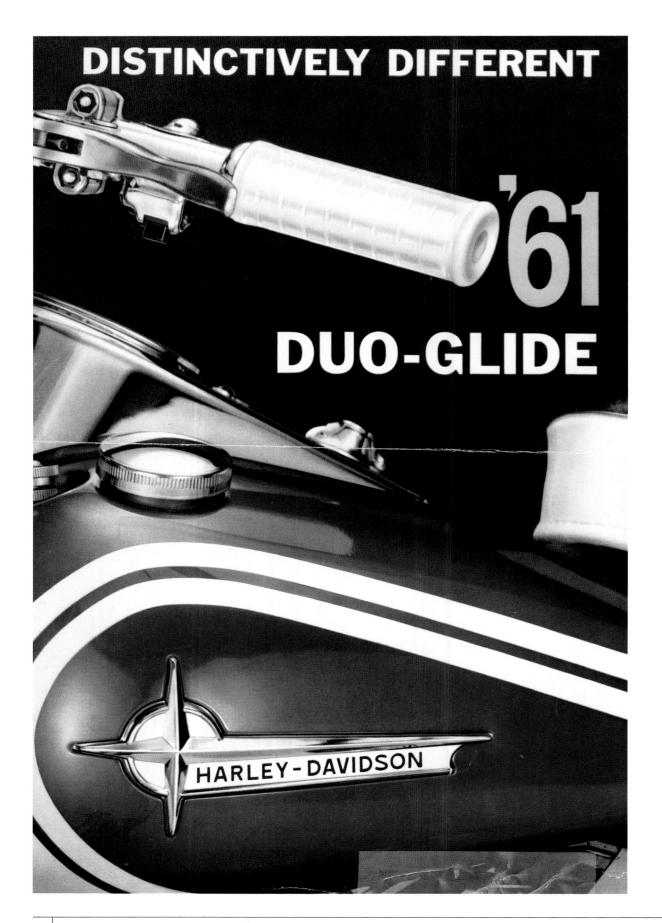

NOW **WAY AHEAD STAY AHEAD** POWER

with the new
HARLEY-DAVIDSON
250cc
Sprint

SEE IT...RIDE IT...TODAY!

1962

To compete with the influx of lightweight motorcycles from Japan, Harley-Davidson began importing 4-stroke singles from its plant in Italy in 1961. In styling, performance, and handling, the 250cc Sprint, with its horizontal cylinder, was a match for its competition. The 1962 Model H, with its high exhaust, was especially attractive to off-road enthusiasts.

1961

Distinctively different in paint scheme only, the 1961 Harley-Davidson models were offered in black and white or red and white with the same optional Hi-Fi colors available the year before. The motorcycle market experienced a slump in the late fifties and early sixties, so it was difficult to justify the cost of dramatic product changes.

1962

Splashes of psychedelic color helped promote Harley-Davidson's playful Topper motor scooter. Available in Tango Red, Skyline Blue, or Granada Green and white, the 1962 Topper was powered by a 165cc 2-stroke single with an automatic drive. It featured larger diameter wheels than contemporary scooters plus a unique hand-pull start.

HARLEY-DAVIDS

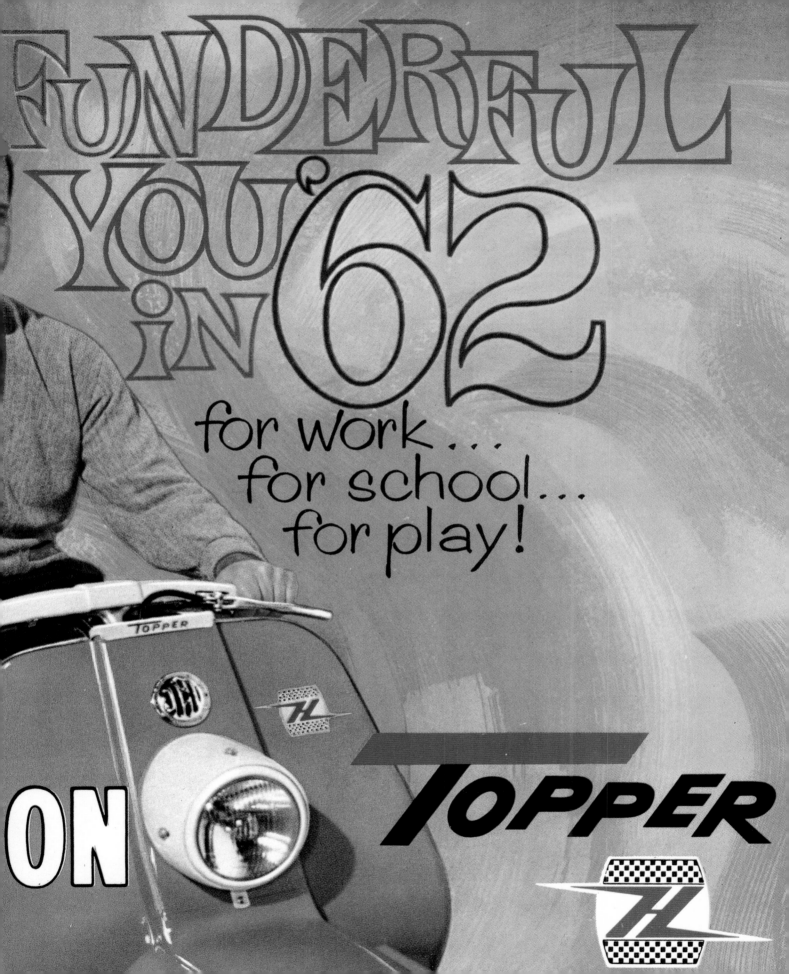

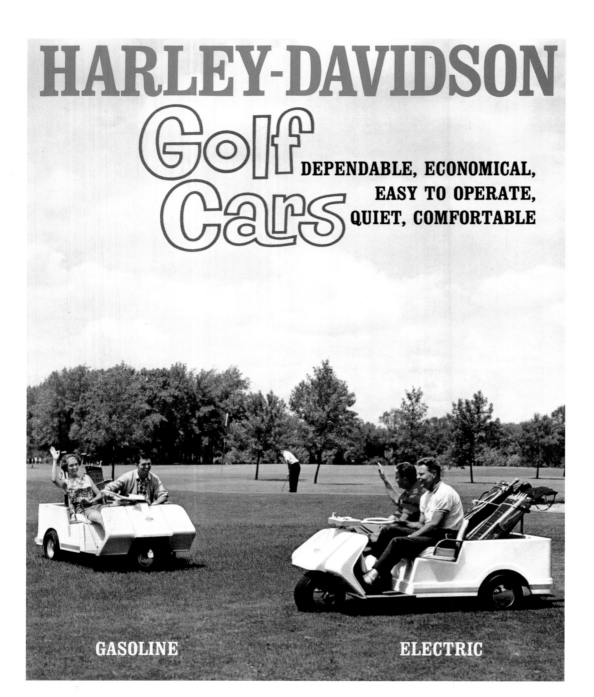

HARLEY-DAVIDSON
Golf Cars
DEPENDABLE, ECONOMICAL, EASY TO OPERATE, QUIET, COMFORTABLE

GASOLINE

ELECTRIC

19**62**

Attempting to broaden and diversify, Harley-Davidson introduced a line of gasoline and electric golf cars in the early sixties, with fiberglass bodies manufactured at the newly acquired plant in Tomahawk, Wisconsin. By the end of the decade, Harley-Davidson accounted for a third of the U.S. golf car business.

19**63**

Despite having lightweight motorcycle offerings from both its American and Italian plants, Harley-Davidson's main emphasis was on the Sportster and Duo-Glide models, with their powerful V-Twin engines. Sales had dropped to an all-time post-depression level by 1963, and Harley-Davidson stressed the joys of two-up touring in order to stimulate sales.

RIDE THE ROAD TO REAL ADVENTURE

NEW FOR '64
HARLEY-DAVIDSON

1964

The freedom of the open road has always been a lure for the Harley-Davidson rider. The entire lineup of 1964 Harley-Davidson motorcycles is depicted in this artist's rendering of a group of riders on a country lane.

19**66**

Harley-Davidson imported a line of lightweight motorcycles, including the 250cc Sprint, built in a subsidiary plant in Varese, Italy. Aermacchi Harley-Davidson marketed a larger and markedly different line of the same model directly to the European market.

19**66**

In 1965, a streamliner powered by a 250cc Sprint engine set a land speed record on the Bonneville Salt Flats and returned a year later to break its own record. The engine used was a racing version of the same one that powered the street models of the Sprint, a fact Harley-Davidson was eager to publicize.

1967

Traditionally known for building large, quality, V-Twin-powered touring and sport motorcycles, Harley-Davidson sought to attract a younger rider to its fold by offering a line of lightweight motorcycles built in its Italian subsidiary plant, Aermacchi Harley-Davidson. Inexpensive to own and operate, they were often presented as being fun vehicles to ride.

1967

The Swinging Sixties were a time of free styles, bright colors, straight hair, and pale lipstick. Harley-Davidson was always quick to incorporate the latest trends into its advertising pieces. The little 65cc singles, with their bright colors and low cost of operation, appealed to the young and hip crowd.

1971

The headline for the 1971 introduction of the Super Glide was meant to evoke a hint of mystery about this first-ever factory custom. The "night train" headline (not pictured here) that originally accompanied this ad was an allusion to a popular song from a few years earlier and was never meant to be the nickname for the motorcycle itself, though many mistakenly called it that.

1970s

1970 (Below and opposite)

Throughout its history, Harley-Davidson has produced posters to advertise its racing victories. In 1970, the posters were few and far between as the Company was forced to race the stopgap iron-head XR-750 because of rule changes. The early XR was fast enough, but often ran too hot to make it to the finish line.

DAVE SEHL WINS
ON HARLEY-DAVIDSON XR 750
LOUISVILLE NATIONAL
HALF-MILE 6/6

GEORGE ROEDER WINS
LOUISVILLE 5 STAR 6/7
ON HARLEY-DAVIDSON XR 750

FOR YOUR COPY OF THIS POSTER NO. 703 SEND $1.00 TO DESK A-6, HARLEY-DAVIDSON MOTOR CO. MILWAUKEE, WIS. 53201   SUBSTITUTION WILL BE MADE IF ORDER DOES NOT SPECIFY POSTER NO. 703 OR IF SUPPLY IS EXHAUSTED. ALLOW 30 DAYS FOR DELIVERY.   SILK SCREEN PRINTED IN U.S.A. 7/70 FM

DAVE SEHL MISCONDUCTS
CHARITY NEWSIES NATIONAL 6/28
AMATEUR WINNER REY BEAUCHAMP

pull the
trigger

1971

The Sportster reigned supreme as the ultimate superbike in the sixties. By 1970, though, its fame as one of the fastest bikes on the road was fading. Nonetheless, the Sportster maintained a well-deserved reputation for delivering arm-wrenching torque and bullet-like acceleration.

You'll never forget your first Harley-Davidson.

Neither will we.

Your first Harley-Davidson—a snowmobile built with a difference. Style that stops your mind. Hot lines, hot performance. An all-new 398cc 2-stroke twin; designed, developed and manufactured by Harley-Davidson.

There's another Harley-Davidson difference, one that can be even more important to you. Most manufacturers started with a machine, and then went looking for dealers. Harley-Davidson began looking for dealers in 1903.

Harley-Davidson owners will never be left out in the cold. We build a quality machine. And put our name and years of experience in recreational vehicles solidly behind it. Trained, qualified dealers. Service and parts, locally available. In snowmobiles—as in motorcycles — Harley-Davidson means performance today. And service tomorrow. AMF | Harley-Davidson, Milwaukee, Wis. 53201.

it's the year of the Harley-Davidson difference.

1972

When Harley-Davidson entered the snowmobile market in 1971, the Company believed its strongest trump card was having an established dealer organization backed by a reputable vehicle manufacturer. The Company hoped first-time snowmobile buyers would liken the experience to that enjoyed by the motorcycle enthusiasts.

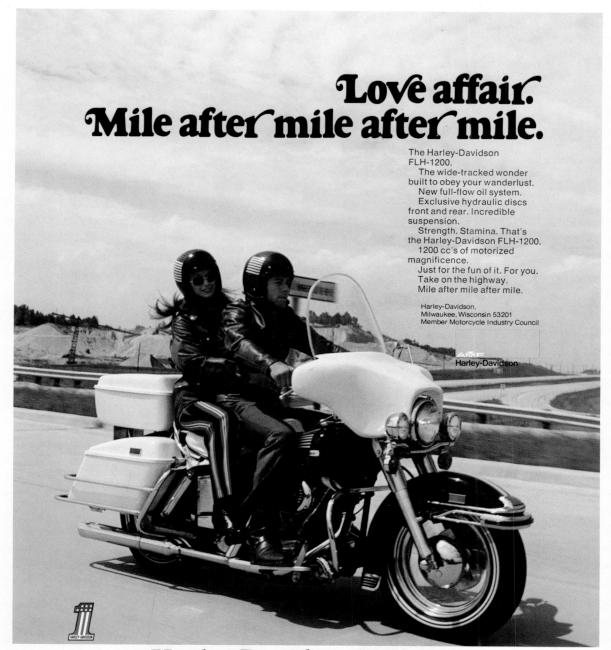

Love affair.
Mile after mile after mile.

The Harley-Davidson
FLH-1200.
The wide-tracked wonder
built to obey your wanderlust.
New full-flow oil system.
Exclusive hydraulic discs
front and rear. Incredible
suspension.
Strength. Stamina. That's
the Harley-Davidson FLH-1200.
1200 cc's of motorized
magnificence.
Just for the fun of it. For you.
Take on the highway.
Mile after mile after mile.

Harley-Davidson,
Milwaukee, Wisconsin 53201
Member Motorcycle Industry Council

AMF
Harley-Davidson

Harley-Davidson FLH-1200.
The Great American Freedom Machine.

1973

Advertised as one of the Great American Freedom Machines™, the 1973
FLH-1200 staked its claim as the ultimate in over-the-road excitement and
touring pleasure. Interestingly, the entire product line was referred to only
by model designation at the time, with product names such as the Electra
Glide having been dropped in favor of letter and number designations.

1975

In the waning years of the Italian lightweight era, Harley-Davidson hoped a sexier image would help sell the 175cc and 250cc two-strokes. With its play on words and models facing off in the desert sun, this 1975 ad presented a hip image of the Company's small model offerings.

ONLY ONE MAN COULD HAVE DONE THIS.

Harley-Davidson's new Cafe Racer couldn't have been built by a committee. There's no compromise.

Only one man could have built the Cafe Racer. Willie G. If he wore a suit, he'd be William G. Davidson. But he doesn't. So he's Willie G., the man who designed the Super Glide, and now, the all-new, 1977 XLCR Cafe Racer.

"I wanted to build the ultimate, no compromise bike. So I built it first, then presented it. Before the presentation, I said to myself, "If they like it, we're going to build it. If they don't, I'll keep it for myself." They liked it.

No wonder. A street legal Cafe Racer in black on black, Willie G.'s creation may be the ultimate customizing job:

He took the engine from the powerful 1977 Sportster. Sculpted the seat and rear end to resemble the famous XR-750 racer. Added a specially-designed gas tank. Put on a unique Siamese exhaust system with all black pipes.

Those pipes, coupled with the Sportster engine, make the Cafe Racer the most powerful production cycle Harley-Davidson has ever built.

Possessed with an ability to compete with the best of Europe's Cafe Racers, it can hustle down a twisting road while providing outstanding handling at high speeds.

And every detail, from the mating of aluminum cast wheels with Goodyear Eagle AT tires, to the positioning of the footpegs and the inclusion of low-profile handlebars, the careful selection of Willie G. You'll find dual front discs matched with a single disc brake in the rear. A blunted, snub-nose, black fairing with a smoke-colored windshield. And everywhere there's black. Black trim, black cases, black horn, air cleaner cover and pipes.

Even the reproduction of the antique Harley-Davidson brass plate on the gas tank comes from the same source. "Why did I go to the old plate? I just like it."

Willie G. built himself a Cafe Racer. Now you can buy it. However, there will only be a limited number available. See your Harley-Davidson dealer for details.

Until you've been on a Harley-Davidson, you haven't been on a motorcyde.

We believe in safety first. Before you start out, light your lights, put on your helmet and watch out for the other guy. Follow owner's manual for maintenance.

1977

Not since the twenties was a company officer thrust into the limelight at Harley-Davidson. In recognition of his growing acclaim in the motorcycle world, coupled with a growing list of striking new models, Willie G. Davidson began to be featured as the prime mover behind creations such the dark and handsome 1977 XLCR Café Racer.

1979 (left)

The gas shortages and rising prices of the mid- to late-seventies led Harley-Davidson to position its motorcycles as economy vehicles. With estimated gas mileage far exceeding even the most frugal of the American subcompacts, the Low Rider® could deliver cheap transportation and be considerably more fun to drive.

In the mid-seventies, Harley-Davidson adopted the eagle as its unofficial mascot (though the earliest usage dated to the thirties). By 1980, artistic versions, including flamed, chromed, traditional, and neon eagles, were incorporated with the corporate logo.

1980s

LOW RIDER. MORE THAN KNEE DEEP IN IRON JUST 27" OFF THE GROUND.

MORE THAN A MACHINE.

THE SPORTSTER. MORE THAN A LEGEND BROUGHT TO LIFE AT EVERY GREEN LIGHT.

MORE THAN A MACHINE.

STRIKE WHILE THE IRON IS HOT.

1980

Harley-Davidson's most radical paint job to date appeared on the 1980 Wide Glide®, a motorcycle as wild as the orange and yellow flames that adorned its tank. With its wide-placed forks, bobtail rear fender and striking paint, the Wide Glide was an instant success with bikers seeking the custom look.

1980

After decades of presenting a squeaky-clean image in its advertising, Harley-Davidson finally acknowledged its core rider by offering ads with a distinct edge. The Low Rider and Sportster are presented here in gritty, realistic settings unlike the race tracks or park-like settings of previous years.

1981

The conglomerate AMF Incorporated owned Harley-Davidson from 1969 to June 1981. During that period, the association was a sore point for Harley-Davidson enthusiasts who wanted the Motor Company to control its own destiny. Riders were thrilled when the news broke that, at last, the eagle soared alone.

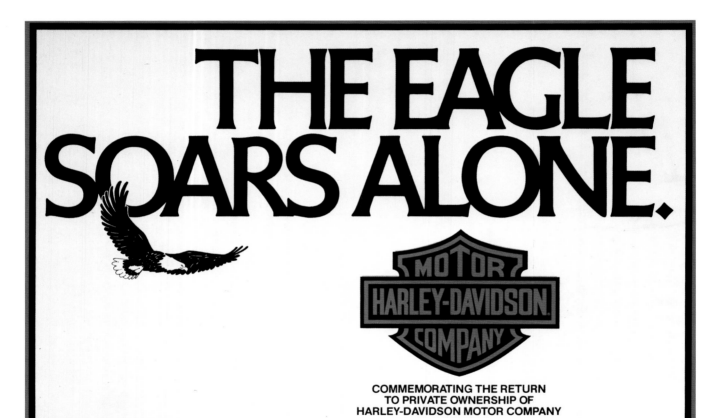

Supplying motorcycles to the nation's police force has been an important part of Harley-Davidson's business strategy since Detroit bought its first fleet in 1908. Many of the Motor Company's engineers, designers, and marketing force were (and continue to be) avid riders who could identify and address the concerns of the mounted officer.

19**83**

As early as 1909, Harley-Davidson Motor Company was running ads decrying the fact that its competitors were copying the design and features of its motorcycles. With the advent of the cruiser class, history soon repeated itself. By 1982, Harley-Davidson was once again producing ads directed at its imitators.

19**82**

Paraphrasing the famous closing of the Gettysburg Address, Harley-Davidson was eager to point out that its motorcycles were designed and built by real motorcyclists, just like the people who bought and rode them. This closeness to the rider has been a recurring theme with the Motor Company since its earliest days.

There had been a long-running perception in the early eighties that certain Harley-Davidson dealers did not want competitive brand motorcycles in their lots, and in some instances, preferred not to sell to their riders. Harley-Davidson sought to make it clear that all motorcyclists shared a common interest and that all were welcome under its Bar & Shield.

Long known for solid, quality construction, the Harley-Davidson motorcycle was a machine for the ages. This philosophy was in marked contrast to that of its overseas competitors, who were burdened with a reputation for building bikes that were more or less interchangeable with one another and somewhat disposable.

1983

The total domination of the nation's dirt tracks by the XR-750 race bike promoted a cry for a street version to rule the asphalt. In 1983, Harley-Davidson debuted the XR-1000, a model with an engine derived from its racing cousin. Despite being billed as the fastest Harley-Davidson street model ever built, the XR was discontinued after only two years.

I AM WOMAN. HEAR ME ROAR.

A woman's place, we all know, is wherever she wants to be. And there's no better way to get there than on a Harley.® So join the club that put the "move" in the women's movement, the Harley Owners Group,® by visiting your local Harley-Davidson® dealer or calling 1 (800) CLUB HOG.★

JOIN THE HARLEY OWNERS GROUP.®

*In Wisconsin 1 (800) 242-2464, in Canada 1 (416) 741-5510.

THANK GOD
THEY DON'T LEAK OIL ANYMORE.

When it comes to motorcycle technology, we've risen to new heights.
THINGS ARE DIFFERENT ON A HARLEY.

WOULD YOU SELL
AN UNRELIABLE MOTORCYCLE
TO THESE GUYS?

We don't.
THINGS ARE DIFFERENT ON A HARLEY.

1986

The Evolution engine forever changed the image of Harley-Davidson motorcycles as being unreliable, oil-leaking machines. This ad, featuring the Heritage Softail®-shaped hot air balloon of U.S. tycoon Malcolm Forbes rising above a sea of onlookers, poked fun at that earlier reputation with tongue-in-cheek good humor.

1987

With its quality problems in the past by 1987 and the corporate bottom line firmly in the black, Harley-Davidson could afford to lampoon its former dubious reputation. It was evident that the new Harley-Davidson motorcycles were far superior in reliability and performance than their predecessors, and the Motor Company was quick to get the word out.

1987

In the seventies, only a tiny fraction of Harley-Davidson riders were women. With the introduction of the cleaner, more reliable Evolution motor in 1984, an increasing number of female enthusiasts bought their own bikes. Just four years later, Harley-Davidson was actively recruiting women to join its factory club, the Harley Owners Group.

You never see an automobile name, or even that of one of Harley-Davidson's competitors, tattooed on the owner's body. This is an honor reserved only for America's premier motorcycle and illustrates the devotion of the rider to the brand and lifestyle.

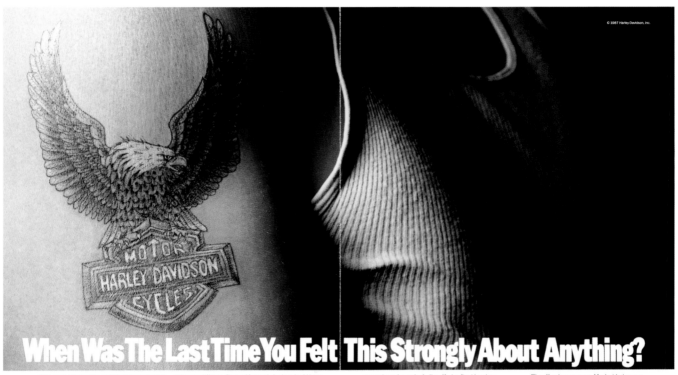

When Was The Last Time You Felt This Strongly About Anything?

Wake up in the morning, and life picks up where it left off. You do what has to be done. Use what it takes to get there. And what once seemed exciting has now become part of the numbing routine. It all begins to feel the same.

Except when you've got a Harley-Davidson.®
Something strikes a nerve. The heartfelt thunder rises up, refusing to become part of the background. Suddenly,

things are different. Clearer. More real. As they should have been all along.

The feeling is personal. It affects everyone a little differently. For some, owning a Harley® is a statement of individuality. For others, owning one means being a part of a home-grown legacy that was born in a tiny Milwaukee shed in 1903. Regardless of the reason, more people

are getting to know the feeling. Harley-Davidson has reemerged as the number one selling brand of super heavyweight motorcycles in the U.S.A.®

To the uninitiated, a Harley-Davidson motorcycle is often associated with a certain look, a certain sound. Anyone who owns one will tell you it's much more than that. Riding a Harley changes you from within.

The effect is permanent. Maybe it's time you started feeling this strongly.

Things Are Different On A Harley™

19 88

This 1988 model reminded riders that life was once less complicated. The Heritage Softail, with its 1950s retro look, offered a return to simpler times and encouraged riders to escape modern complexities by indulging in a simple pleasure—riding a Harley.

Life Should Be So Simple.

There was a time in nearly everyone's life when the most important things were the essentials—food, shelter and clothing. Things a person can't do without. For more than a few motorcycle riders, the list was one item longer. A Harley-Davidson® was an absolute necessity.

Everyone had all kinds of reasons for why their Harley® was so important. The sound. The made-in-Milwaukee style. And of course, the feeling of owning the road. Today, one Harley in particular brings it all together. The Heritage Softail® Classic.

It evokes a time when all a rider needed was a Hydra Glide™ and a road. The styling is pure Harley classic, with two-tone paint, leather bags, and brilliant chrome. The V² Evolution® engine is a treat for the eyes. And the ears. The sound is honest, powerful, and about as straightforward as it gets.

There might be some point in your life when you just can't do without a Harley-Davidson. Don't be surprised.

It may come soon, spurred on by the thought of a roof over your head, a full 'fridge, and the Heritage Softail Classic. It should be so simple.

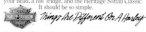

We support the MSF and recommend you wear a helmet and protective gear while riding.

19 89 (Next Page)

Many Harley-Davidson enthusiasts have been riding for decades. Some are second-, third-, or even fourth-generation Harley riders. As this ad so poignantly points out, motorcycling is more than just a sport—it is a way of life that involves and encompasses the whole family.

When Did It Start For You?

Maybe it was the first time you heard one, as the sound entered your ears and reached all the way in until you could feel it in the pit of your stomach. Or maybe it was the first time you knelt down and lost yourself in your own liquid reflection in a stretch of chromed steel. Maybe it was yesterday. Maybe before you can remember. It doesn't matter. Sometime, somehow, it started. The urge to have a Harley-Davidson® took hold. And from that point on, you were very different.

It didn't stop there. The feeling kept after you, like a song you couldn't get out of your head, tugging at you until you did something about it. Maybe you worked a little harder or a little longer. Refigured some priorities. Whatever it took. Until the day came when, finally, you settled

into the seat of your very own Harley.® Still it didn't stop.

You were all the way in. A Harley-Davidson owner. You became part of a home-grown legend, and a unique way of looking at the world. You bought into a philosophy that translates into motorcycles that rise above mere machinery. Motorcycles that don't answer to simple logic. And don't lend themselves to complicated explanation.

If you own one, no doubt you understand.

Maybe you were made to be a Harley owner. Maybe you were born to be one. When did it all start? Only one person can answer that question.

HARLEY-DAVIDSON MOTOR COMPANY

Things Are Different On A Harley.

19**88**

Harley-Davidson celebrated its eighty-fifth anniversary in grand fashion by renting a festival grounds on the shore of Lake Michigan and hosting tens of thousands of Harley-Davidson enthusiasts from all over the world at a day-long party that featured good food, rousing music, and the camaraderie of motorcycling.

1989

What greater call to action could there possibly be than a patriotic appeal from the nation's symbolic uncle? As the sole remaining American motorcycle manufacturer in 1989, this was a clear request to the nation's riders to support America's motorcycle.

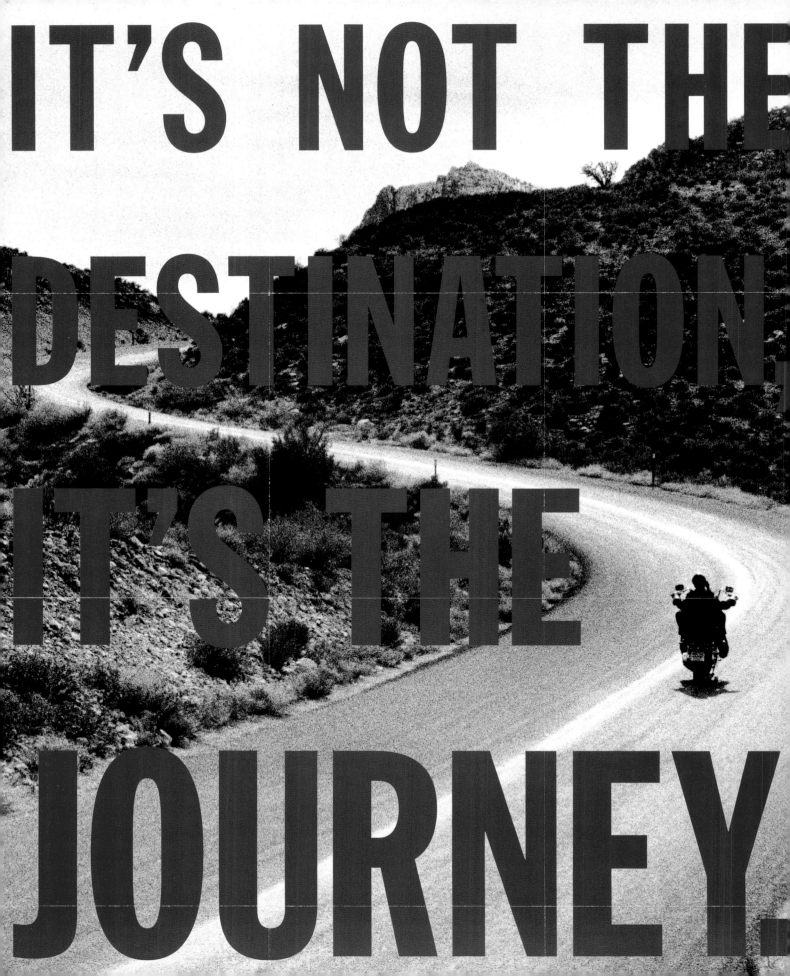

Some say getting there is half the fun, but actually, it's all the fun to Harley-Davidson riders. Whether out for an afternoon ride or touring cross country, the thrill of experiencing the open road on a Harley-Davidson motorcycle in the company of friends is the greatest thrill in motorcycling.

1990s
and Beyond

At six hundred and fifty pounds, who'd dare call it a scooter?

Make way. Because here comes 650 pounds of Harley-Davidson® factory custom. The Fat Boy.®

Scooter, nothing. You're looking at a whole lot of Harley.® From the front wheel to the back, and everything in between, the Fat Boy is a motorcycle that gives new meaning to the word solid.

It's powered by 80 cubic inches worth of black-and-chrome V² Evolution® engine. The Big Twin feeds a shotgun-style dual exhaust system, finished in brilliant chrome just to let everyone know where the rumble is coming from.

The Fat Boy abounds in custom details. Leading the way is an outsized 7-inch chrome headlight only a Harley® of this magnitude could carry off. Just below, you've got a metal front fender, cut back to show off the rubber. Bringing up the rear is a hidden suspension system that delivers a smooth ride while looking for all the world like a true hard tail. On to some of the finer points. Like the genuine leather gas tank trim leading into a textured leather seat insert. And the special leather seat valance, finished with hand lacing. But it's not all there just for good looks.

Sit down and get ready to clear a path. First thing you'll notice is the nostalgic sweep of the honest-to-fifties FLH handlebar. Your boots rest on full-sized floorboards. There is nothing subtle about this motorcycle.

After all, this is no ordinary motorcycle. This is Harley-Davidson, big time. It may be a bit much for some. That's fine. The Fat Boy was never meant for the masses. Hook up with this heavyweight, and you might notice that wherever you go, people give it room.

Where does a 650-pound Fat Boy sit? Anywhere you want.

Through and Through.

It's not the town as much as the horse you rode in on.

Like a free-ranging Badlands spirit, it came and went.

And wherever it went, it brought a piece of Black Hills mystique from the town that gave it a name. The Harley-Davidson® Sturgis. And when it seemed to roll off into the distance for the last time, there were still those who awaited a time when it would return.

Now is that time. The Sturgis is back, looking for all the world as if it had never gone.

Long-time Harley® riders will recognize it immediately and yet not truly know it. Because there has never been another motorcycle, Harley-Davidson or otherwise, like the new Sturgis. Beneath its black-as-sin paint lies new-from-the-ground-up technology. It starts with the Dyna Glide™ chassis. While it looks to be a dead ringer for the one from the original Sturgis, this frame features a new two-point engine isolation mounting system. Which makes it one of the best-riding Harleys ever. It's also one of the most finely detailed Harleys ever. For example, check out the new oil tank. Its location is not only convenient, it allows for shorter, more tucked-in oil lines for a cleaner look. Then there's the hidden exhaust crossover that fully exposes the 80 cubic inch Evolution® engine, finished in black. And like the original, the new Sturgis moves down the road with a final belt drive system that is clean, strong and quiet.

This is a motorcycle that will bring to any town the mystery of the country that inspired it and the town that named it.

A motorcycle bound by the script found next to its rider's knee. Sturgis. And just as the faithful have returned to the town every year, now at last, the motorcycle has been returned to the faithful.

Through and Through.

1990

As Harley-Davidson's dominance of the U.S. motorcycle market accelerated, the Motor Company could adopt a saucy, flippant attitude in its advertising, secure in its popularity.

When was the last time you met a stranger and knew he was a brother?

A chance meeting on the highway turns into an immediate connection.

The glimmer of recognition between two people who are not just passing strangers. Two Harley® riders.

If you're one of these riders, you know: The two of you have been through quite a few of the same things. Like going out for a quick morning ride and not coming back until dark. Following a squiggly line on a map just for the pure fun of it. Forgetting to stop and eat. Common experiences that become a shared obsession.

It's this kind of obsession that inspired the Harley-Davidson® FXR series—The Super Glide®, the Low Riders® and the Sport Glide®. Six different Harleys that share a common mission. Putting a rider at one with the road. They have a go-anywhere versatility that takes them from short cruise to long haul without ever missing a beat. A lot of that versatility comes from a sport chassis and a 39mm fork that allows both stability and sure handling. Which means that any FXR is as much at home on the interstate as it is on a winding back road. At the heart of it all is the 80 cubic inch Evolution® engine, isolation-mounted for a smooth and comfortable ride. Famous for its look and sound as much as for its ground-gobbling torque, the Big Twin will move you in ways you'd never imagined.

When you ride a Harley for the first time, something clicks. You won't look at another Harley rider as a stranger again. Because chances are, that is where your first on-the-road thumbs up is coming from.

You'll understand. It means "way to go." It means you've got more in common than bug-splattered leathers.

It means welcome to the family.

Through and Through.

What's the last thing to go through a june bug's mind?

"Nice Harley." A rider might hardly notice; it's just another smudge on the windshield. Besides, there's a whole lot of road to be ridden up ahead. Even more so when the machine between the rider and the road is a motorcycle built to remain in motion. The Low Rider® Convertible™ is a Harley-Davidson® that just doesn't sit still for very long. And that means bad news for the insect population.

Like all FXR-series Harleys, the Convertible's horizon-chasing motivation comes from the 1340cc V² Evolution® engine, isolation-mounted for a smooth ride.

Beyond that, the frame adds to the motorcycle's capabilities by delivering a confidence-building combination of straight-line stability and solid cornering. It's matched to an air adjustable anti-dive front fork. The suspension at both ends was designed with cornering clearance in mind, and you'll notice that there was no skimping on the rubber, either. The Convertible rolls on Dunlop® Elite tires.

If this Harley sounds like a machine built for sport, you're only about half right. It'll handle the sedate pace of an arrow-straight four-lane as well as it handles curves. With its wide seat, spacious riding position and Lexan® windshield, it's comfortable enough for serious saddle time.

And once you hit town, it's also got the style for not-so-serious saddle time. The windshield and saddlebags are mounted with quick-disconnect hardware. They come off in a matter of minutes, and—surprise—the Convertible gets down to the lean, clean lines of a Harley-Davidson Low Rider.

Which, you'll find, is just the ticket for a night on the boulevard. After all, even the most high-mileage wind addict knows there's more to riding than collecting bugs.

Through and Through.

1990–91

Humor and the camaraderie of the open road have been recurring themes in Harley-Davidson advertising, reminders that the sport is intended to be enjoyable and fun.

Harley-Davidson riders have always been a breed that seeks the road less trav-
eled. In 1992, Harley-Davidson asked riders what would they rather be doing
if they didn't have to deal with the demands of everyday life. Freedom from
the cares of the modern world and a new Heritage Softail summed it up
nicely for most.

IF YOU DIDN'T HAVE TO ANSWER TO ANYONE, WHAT WOULD YOU DO?

Responsibility can get pretty heavy at times. There are bills to pay, appointments to keep, time clocks to punch. Always someone looking over your shoulder. Sometimes it can feel like you're on a short leash with a tight collar. If you could do something just because you wanted to do it, would you? At Harley-Davidson, we did. One look at the Heritage Softail' Classic could tell you that. This is a motorcycle that has nothing to do with the daily grind. It was made for fun. If you doubt that, take a listen to the Evolution' Big Twin as it sings of good times in the great unknown. It has a special ability to pull you farther and farther away from anything resembling the rat race. Machines like this don't just happen. But in building the Heritage Softail Classic, we really had to answer only to ourselves. Maybe it's time you thought about doing the same thing.

Through and Through.

We care about you. Sign up for a Motorcycle Safety Foundation rider course today. Ride with your headlight on and watch out for the other person. Always wear a helmet, proper eyewear and appropriate clothing, and insist your passenger does too. Protect your privilege to ride by joining the American Motorcyclist Association. © 1992 Harley-Davidson, Inc. Call 1-800-443-2153 for the location of a Harley-Davidson' dealer near you.

Harley Owners Group®, or H.O.G.®, was founded in 1983 in order to bring Harley riders together to share riding experiences. With over 600,000 members, it's the largest motorcycle organization in the world.

The best meetings we have take place under an open sky. Riding is what the Harley Owners Group® is about.

It's an organization of more than 225,000 individuals who believe that the important thing is to be out there in the wind.

A one-year membership is automatic when you buy a new Harley-Davidson.®

Whether it's a local ride or an annual event such as our regional and national H.O.G.® rallies, you'll have plenty of chances to get in the saddle and go.

Of course, there are fringe benefits, too.

As a member, you'll receive a H.O.G. pin, patch, membership card and touring handbook, along with a subscription to Hog Tales® magazine. You'll also have access to our Fly & Ride™ program, emergency pick-up service and more.

Your Harley-Davidson dealer can fill you in on all the details, or you can learn more by calling 1-800-CLUB-HOG.

If you've got what it takes to get in, namely a Harley-Davidson motorcycle, you're on your way.

1 9 0 3 H A R L E Y - D A V I D S O N 1 9 9 3

· 1 9 9 3 M O T O R C Y C L E S ·

19**93**

Celebrating its ninetieth birthday in 1993, Harley-Davidson called attention
to its history and heritage by picturing a replica of a 1903 model on the cover
of its prestige literature. Several of the anniversary models sported special
two-tone paint and cloisonné tank badges commemorating the event.

HARLEY-DAVIDSON®

1994 MOTORCYCLES

1994

Wide-open spaces and Harley-Davidson have always gone together. The launch of the Road King® introduced a new element to sport touring with its FL power train in a stripped-down, sportier chassis and ample chrome.

GRANDPA WAS A KNUCKLEHEAD.

1994

The overhead valve Big Twin, here pictured as a 1994 Road King, had its origins in the Knucklehead engine of 1936. This ad pays playful homage to the fact that, decades later, the lineage is clearly defined.

The boss's thumb don't reach this far.

1994

With the pressures of the modern workplace sometimes difficult to escape, Harley-Davidson riders had a friend in the Dyna Wide Glide. Wide-spaced forks graced by a twenty-one-inch laced wheel, apehanger bars, forward controls, and a bobtail rear fender all combined to deliver the rider to a place on the open road not even the boss could reach.

Just released. The Harley-Davidson Bad Boy.

1995

Not many companies would dare to introduce a bike so bad that it featured a prison in its ad. The 1995 Bad Boy®, with its all-black Springer front end, had the kind of attitude that only Harley-Davidson could successfully bring to market at the time.

"My older brother has a Harley. Mom told me his name is Dave."

1998

The Harley rider's passion for the open road is poignantly underscored with this imaginary, plaintive comment from a sibling whose older brother is traveling the nation's highways and byways.

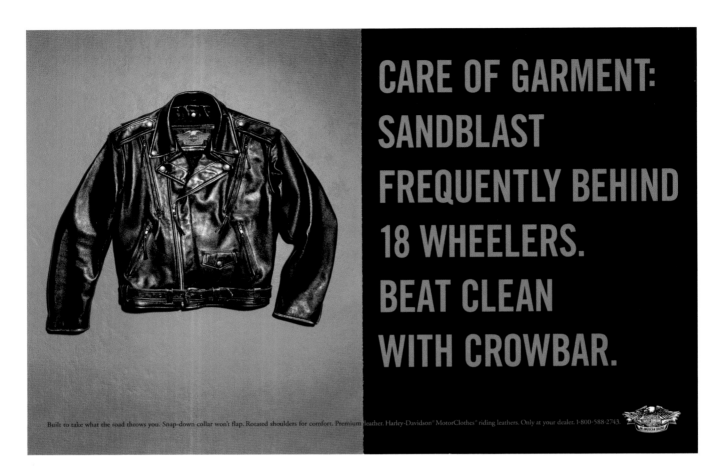

CARE OF GARMENT: SANDBLAST FREQUENTLY BEHIND 18 WHEELERS. BEAT CLEAN WITH CROWBAR.

Built to take what the road throws you. Snap-down collar won't flap. Rotated shoulders for comfort. Premium leather. Harley-Davidson® MotorClothes® riding leathers. Only at your dealer. 1-800-588-2743.

1998

Harley-Davidson has been selling clothing for motorcyclists since 1911, and its reputation for providing quality garments that combine fashion with function has become legendary. As this ad from 1998 points out, its motorcycle jackets are made to take all that miles on the road can dish out.

YOU COMMIT 4 OF THE 7 DEADLY SINS JUST LOOKING AT IT.

Behold the cutting edge of Harley-Davidson styling. Pure tradition, in a place it's never been. Note the clean front end, stretched fuel tank and rear fender (Lust). Check the steel hoses, small turn signals and recessed taillight (Envy). The look would put a show bike to shame (Pride). At the center is a twin balanced, Twin Cam 88B™ engine (Gluttony). The Softail® Deuce.™ Call 1-800-443-2153 or visit www.harley-davidson.com for a dealer. The Legend Rolls On.™

1999

Harley-Davidson motorcycles generate strong emotions in those who ride and enjoy them. Just looking at their sculpted chrome and steel adorned with stunning paint brings forth irrational thoughts that transcend what noninitiates would consider normal.

20**00**

Only Harley-Davidson can get away with poking good-natured fun at a name
it conceived. Since its introduction in 1990, the Fat Boy has been one of
Harley-Davidson's most popular models and the object of motorcycling
desire for more than a decade.

INSIDE EVERY MAN THERE'S A FAT BOY TRYING TO GET OUT.

It's in you, all right. A Fat Boy? Or a Sportster® or Wide Glide® or Road King® Chromed steel and perfect paint and when you hit the starter it takes you into the wind where it's all good. Well, don't let too much more life slip by before you let it out. In this world, time you miss is time you don't get back. 1-800-443-2153 or www.harley-davidson.com. **The Legend Rolls On.™**

20**02**

On any given morning, a few gallons of gas and a Harley-Davidson Road King Classic are all anyone needs to escape the constraints of the modern world. A turn of the key and a flick of the wrist send the rider to the open road, where nothing matters but the hum of the tires on the pavement and the miles of scenery rolling by.

ROAD KING CLASSIC. 8 A.M. ONE TANKFUL FROM CIVILIZATION.

20**02** (Next Page)

After ninety-nine years, Harley-Davidson seemed rock-solid in its dedication to the 45-degree, air-cooled, V-Twin engine that had been its trademark since 1909. The 2002 V-Rod, with its 60-degree liquid-cooled Revolution engine, shook the foundations of the motorcycling world as the centerpiece of a radically different machine that was still Harley-Davidson at its core.

Always wear a helmet.

We care about you. Sign up for a Motorcycle Safety Foundation rider course today (for a course near you call 1-800-446-9227). Ride safely and within the limits of the law and your abilities. Ride with your headlight on. Watch out for the other person. Always wear a helm

99 YEARS OF WIND CAN CHANGE TH

The world spins. Time marches on. But as always, we use the bedrock of tradition to push our designs. Take a look at our latest: the Harley-Davidson® V-Rod™ motorcycle. Traffic-stopping style. Long, raked-out front end.